CONTENTS

GENERAL LEARNING OBJECTIVES OF THIS UNIT

This Open Learning Unit will supply you with all the core information you need to answer an examination question or to write an essay on perception. It will take you about 4 to 5 hours to work through. You are advised to try as many of the 'Something to Try' and 'Possible Projects' as time allows, as these will help you to remember the information. If you attempt all these activities, it might well take you longer to complete the Unit.

By the end of this Unit, you should:

▷ have an overview of the complex area of perception and, in particular, of visual perception;

▷ understand how a sensory experience becomes a meaningful perception;

▷ be familiar with the theories which attempt to explain how we recognize objects and people;

▷ and be able to relate this knowledge about visual perception to the nature-nurture debate.

What is Perception?

The world around us is full of meaning. It is important for our everyday life, even for our very survival, to make sense of it all. For example, if you were in North Queensland, Australia, and you were about to wade across a river, how would you be able to tell whether the object you could see in the water was a crocodile or a harmless log? Or, closer to home, how do you decide if it is safe to cross the road when there is a car travelling towards you?

Have you ever been challenged by someone who says that you looked right through them when you were out shopping? Assuming that you have no sight problems, you must have 'seen' them and yet they didn't register in your brain. Or perhaps you have lost something, and hunted high and low, only to find it was right under your nose. If you have ever watched a film sequence shot from the front of a roller-coaster and felt your stomach lurch, and your back push into your seat against the drop, you have experienced another intriguing facet of perception — it is much more than the mere use of the senses.

How can we define perception?

Perception involves the taking in of information, through our senses, and then processing that information to make meaningful sense of it all.

When you come to think about this it is an amazing process. You will probably have watched a 'whodunnit' on television or at the cinema and been irritated to find in the usual flashback sequence, when the murderer is revealed, that you 'missed' an important clue. You **saw** everything on the screen, and yet you did not **perceive** the all-important piece of evidence.

Below is a copy of the lithograph 'Waterfall' by M.C. Escher.

FIGURE 1. *Escher's 'Waterfall'.* © 1961 M.C. Escher/Cordon Art-Baarn-Holland.

At first sight it's just a picture of a waterfall powering a waterwheel. But if you now LOOK at the picture you will realize that it's an impossible figure. The water appears to be flowing uphill, and the supporting pillars of the aqueduct could not have been built as they appear to be. Clearly, seeing and looking are not the same thing. If you are a competition entrant you will have spent at least some of your time looking for ten differences between picture A and picture B, a task which seems simple but is actually very difficult. So perceiving is not simply experiencing sensations.

This Unit will introduce you to the complicated mechanisms which make perception the active (not at all passive) process that it is. Perception is **selective, constructive** and **interpretative** — as we can show by examining your perception of the Escher picture. What went 'wrong' with your perception? First, you would have selected which aspects of the picture to attend to. As the falling water and the waterwheel dominate the central area of the picture, your eye (and brain) select them (as the artist intended) and you are misled by them. You then take in the tower-like constructions and construct them into what seems to be a sensible arrangement; and it is at this point you might have stopped and felt something was amiss. This is the moment when you begin to ascribe meaning to the picture, but the only possible interpretation is that the water is flowing UPHILL! All your education and experiences tell you that water can't do this, and so you look for another interpretation, and the artist's 'trick' is exposed.

Part of the difficulty with this painting is that Escher plays with your expectations. To demonstrate the fact that we frequently perceive what we expect to perceive, what do you see in Figure 2?

It is likely that you report seeing 'Once upon a time', when in fact what is written is 'Once upon a a time'.

Perception, then, does not depend entirely on the information that is present; it is biased by 'the expectations, hopes, fears, needs and memories that make up our internal world' (Barber and Legge, 1976).

Although many different writers use different terms to describe how our internal world affects our perception, in this Unit Allport's (1955) term set* will be used because the name itself describes its nature. The different factors which determine our perceptual set will be considered later in the Unit.

ONCE

UPON A

A TIME

FIGURE 2

1 The Sensory Processes

KEY AIMS: By the end of this section you should:

▷ *appreciate how light entering the eye forms an image, which is converted into a pattern of electrical activity in nerve cells*

▷ *comprehend the importance of absolute and difference thresholds in signal detection*

▷ *understand how colour vision works.*

Before we can make sense of the world we have to begin by taking in the range of information around us through our senses.

There are five basic senses:

> sight
> hearing
> touch
> taste
> smell.

In addition, we have a kinaesthetic sense*, which informs us of the position of our body and movements of parts of the body. This is a sense we take somewhat for granted. However, if you have ever tried to walk when your foot has 'gone to sleep' you will realize how difficult movement is without information about the foot's contact with the floor.

It is kinaesthesis which helps us to keep our balance when walking or riding a bike, and it also helps us when we grasp or manipulate objects, for example the deceptively heavy weight which has to be lifted with greater effort while bracing the back.

Although much of the information in this Unit applies to all six senses, vision is a particularly important sense for humans and so we will concentrate on sight.

Sensory System — The Eye

FIGURE 3 is a diagram of the pathway of light into the eye.

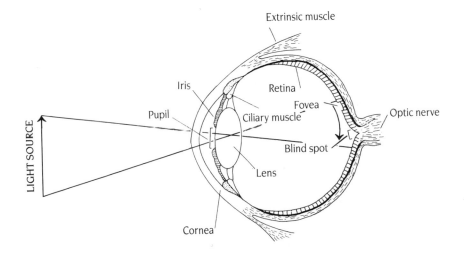

3

The various parts of the eye have different functions:

pupil	determines the amount of light entering the eye
iris	(the coloured part of the eye) has tiny muscles that contract and dilate the pupil
cornea	focuses the incoming light to form an image on the retina
lens	also contributes to focusing light; the curvature of the lens can change in a process known as accommodation*
retina	is a delicate membrane with three layers of neural cells: receptor cells (rods* and cones*), bipolar cells and ganglion cells
fovea	the region where in daylight the most finely detailed vision is possible
blind spot	exactly what its name suggests — no receptor cells are found here.

The blind spot is where the optic nerve leaves the eye and so there are no receptor cells. Normally this creates no problems for us because our eyes are moving and one eye covers what the other one misses, but you can demonstrate its existence for yourself with the aid of Figure 4.

SPOT   **DOG**

FIGURE 4. *Demonstration of the effect of the blind spot.*

 SOMETHING TO TRY

Close your left eye and look at the SPOT. Then move the page to within nine inches or so of your face and the DOG will disappear.

Light enters the eye through the pupil which contracts or dilates according to the movement of the muscles in the iris. In normal vision, the light passes through the lens and the image of the object falls upon the retina. In short-sighted people the focus of a distant object is in front of the retina and so vision is blurred; and in long-sighted people an object would come into focus behind the retina, resulting also in blurred vision.

Gregory (1966) has estimated that about 90% of light entering the eye is absorbed by structures other than the retina. The remaining 10% reaches the receptor cells, the rods and cones. Each rod or cone generates a tiny electrical signal which is proportional to the brightness of light.

Rods and cones

If you think for a moment about what happens when you come home late at night and the house is dark, you will be able to appreciate the importance of the rods. You leave the street lights and enter into the blackness. At first you can see nothing, but even as you fumble for the light switch you begin to make out shapes. It is the rods which are responsible for this ability to see in the dark. Rods are more sensitive than cones, and there are about 120 million of them distributed fairly evenly around the retina. They respond to dim light, when the pupil dilates to allow more light to enter the eye. It takes about 20 minutes before your eyes are maximally sensitive.

Cones allow you to see colour. There are about 6 million of them and they are concentrated in and around the fovea.

Q. Knowing what you do about the eye, can you work out two reasons why cats are better at night vision than humans?

A. One reason is because a cat's pupils can open much more widely than ours can. The other reason is that they have a higher proportion of rods so that their dark vision is more effective, but this has the result that they can't see details or colour as well as humans (Moser, 1987).

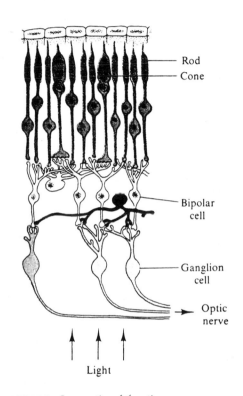

FIGURE 5. *Cross-section of the retina.*

Figure 5 shows how the information from the many millions of rods and cone cells activates bipolar cells which then pass the information to the one million ganglion cells which comprise the optic nerve. In other words, some processing goes on before the information reaches the brain.

Absolute Thresholds

We are amazingly sensitive to certain stimuli: a wasp landing on our cheek, a watch ticking in a silent room. An awareness of these very faint stimuli illustrates the absolute threshold*. This is the term used to describe the minimum amount of stimulation needed for a particular stimulus (light, sound, pressure, smell, taste) to be detected 50% of the time.

There is no single, fixed threshold for signal detection* because detecting any weak stimulus depends on a combination of the signal strength (e.g. a tone in a hearing test), your psychological state (your perceptual set — expectations, motivation, experience) and your level of arousal/fatigue.

If you were an air traffic controller and you had to monitor closely blips on a radar screen, you can appreciate how important any variation in your signal detecting ability could be for all the passengers whose flights you are monitoring. The evidence suggests that 30 minutes at such a task is about the limit to ensure maximum vigilance, although this time limit is affected by the time of day, the task itself and even whether people are given a chance to exercise (Warm and Dember, 1986).

Difference Thresholds

We not only need to be able to detect important stimuli, but also to be able to detect small changes in the sights, sounds, smells, tastes, and textures that make up our world. If you play a musical instrument you have to be able to detect very slight discrepancies in the instrument's tuning if you intend to play your best.

The difference threshold* (sometimes called the just noticeable difference, or jnd) is the minimum difference a person can reliably detect between any two

5

stimuli. The difference threshold varies with the magnitude of the stimulus. For example, you would probably be able to detect 1 gram added to a 10 gram weight, but you would not be so likely to detect 1 gram added to a 1 kilogram weight.

Weber's Law states that the difference threshold, rather than being a constant amount, differs in some constant proportion of the stimulus. Some common difference thresholds are listed in Table 1.

TABLE 1. Common difference thresholds

To be experienced by a typical person as a jnd,

TWO	solutions	must vary in	saltiness	by	8%
	lights		intensity		8%
	objects		weight		2%
	sounds		intensity		5%
	sounds		frequency		0.3%

SOMETHING TO TRY

Below is a computer generated version of Psalm 23. From line to line the typeface changes slightly. How many lines does it take before you can detect a difference?

The LORD is my shepherd;
I shall not want.
He maketh me to lie down
in green pastures:
he leadeth me
beside the still waters.
He restoreth my soul:
he leadeth me
in the paths of righteousness
for his name's sake.
Yea, though I walk through the valley
of the shadow of death,
I will fear no evil:
for thou art with me;
thy rod and thy staff
they comfort me.
Thou preparest a table before me
in the presence of mine enemies:
thou anointest my head with oil,
my cup runneth over.
Surely goodness and mercy
shall follow me
all the days of my life:
and I will dwell
in the house of the LORD
for ever.

D.B. Knuth © 1982 by Visible Language, Rhode Island School of Design

There is more to visual processing in the brain than detecting the brightness of light.

You will remember that signals from the receptors in the eye feed into approximately one million optic nerve fibres. If you look at Figure 6 you will see how information received by each eye is divided, and the half of the retina closest to the nose sends its information through the optic chiasma to the opposite hemisphere, while the information received by the half of the retina nearest to the ears travels to the hemisphere on the same side.

If you look at a person sitting on your immediate left (without turning your head) all the information to be processed about that person's image will be processed in the right hemisphere. This is because for the left eye, the image will fall on the retina closest to the nose, and for the right eye, on the retina closest to the ear. The left hemisphere is not involved at all.

Someone who has brain damage to the visual cortex of one hemisphere will have blind areas in both eyes but, provided that only a part of the cortex is damaged, they will not be completely blind in either eye.

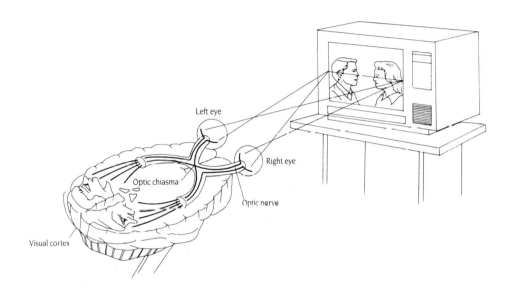

FIGURE 6. *The visual pathway from eye to brain.*

Explain why damage to the right visual cortex does not result in blindness in the right eye.

Colour Vision

The electrical signals produced by the receptor cells are not only influenced by the brightness of the light falling on them, but also by its wavelength. One particular peak wavelength gives the strongest response, while others give gradually weaker responses the further they are in the spectrum from the peak. The human eye has three types of cone cell, and each has a different peak wavelength. These lie in the red, green and blue regions of the spectrum.

Any coloured (chromatic) light reaching your eye is made up of a mixture of different wavelengths, and their proportions determine the colour of the light. For example, the light reflected from a purple crocus in the garden would contain more red and blue light, and less green and yellow. Red and blue sensitive cones will respond strongly to this light, but green sensitive cones will respond weakly.

Trichromatic Theory

This theory of cone cell response is called the Young-Helmholtz Trichromatic Theory* after the two psychologists who developed it. It is the same principle that governs the colour on a colour television set which is based on the mixing of the three primary colours (red, green and blue) on the same additive principle. The complementary colours are produced by mixing colours in pairs.

7

Yellow is formed from the combination of red and green; magenta by mixing red and blue; and cyan by mixing green and blue. All three primary colours together result in white, and black is the absence of any colour.

Opponent Process Theory

A second theory of colour vision is Hering's Opponent Process* Theory. Hering observed that if we see yellow as a result of stimulation of the red sensitive and green sensitive cones, people who are red-green colour blind should not be able to see yellow; and yet they often can.

Hering agreed that three types of cell exist, but he argued that each could respond in two different ways, depending upon the light reaching it. These opposing effects would be produced by:

Cell type 1	red and green
Cell type 2	blue and yellow
Cell type 3	brightness and darkness.

This theory explains what are termed 'negative after effects'.

EG: *If you were to stare at a green square for a while and then look away to a white sheet of paper, you would see a square in green's opponent colour, red.*

According to Hering, this occurs because some substance builds up in red-green opponent cells when they are exposed to green light and is broken down when they are exposed to red light; the after-image is the result of the high level of this substance.

DeValois and DeValois (1975) demonstrated the opponent-processes in monkeys when they measured the activity of single neurons in the area of the brain known as the thalamus* (where impulses from the retina are relayed to the visual cortex) and showed that some neurons are turned 'on' by green and 'off' by red, and others turn off for green and on for red.

Q. Which theory is correct, Young-Helmholtz or Hering?

A. The evidence supports both. It appears that colour processing occurs in two stages.

First, the retinal cone cells do respond in varying degrees to different colours, as the Young-Helmholtz Theory suggested and this is the first stage of colour processing. At a second stage, the signals from these cells are processed by the nervous system's opponent-process cells on the way to the visual cortex. Hering predicted the course of colour vision correctly, and Young-Helmholtz explained the structures.

'Colour blindness'

About 8% of the male population is affected by some form of 'colour blindness' or deficiency in the ability to distinguish colours. Colour blindness* is much less common in females (less than 1%), and is found in a variety of forms. The most common form involves some difficulty in distinguishing red from green, and the causes are now believed to be an abnormality in the red or green sensitive cones, or the absence of one of these cone types. Complete inability to discriminate colours (monochromatic vision) is very much rarer, occurring in less than 1 in 40,000 people, and is thought to be caused by the absence of two, or even all three, types of cone cells.

How do the current theories explain the processes of colour vision?

The human eye and the camera are often compared with each other. How far does this comparison hold true?

From Sensation to Perception

KEY AIMS: By the end of this section you should:

▷ *be able to explain how we obtain information about distance through vision, and the part played in this by binocular vision*

▷ *understand how we perceive movement*

▷ *be familiar with theories of perceptual organization*

▷ *understand what both constancies and illusions tell us about normal vision.*

Perception involves rather more than mere sensory experiences. The retina extracts simple information about brightness and wavelength from a visual array and sends it on to the brain, but there are many visual phenomena which demonstrate that our perceptions are not determined by such simple sensory information alone. Instead, the information must be interpreted by the brain. Just how we perceive the world in three dimensions, how we perceive motion, how we recognize the same object from different angles, and how we perceive constancies in the face of contradictory sensory data, will be considered in this section.

Distance Perception

You might well ask yourself why we need *two* eyes. There are several reasons, but the principal ones have to do with providing us with depth and distance cues. The image that falls on the retina is two-dimensional and yet we perceive the world as having depth. How does this happen? It certainly puzzled the early theorists, and in fact scientifically-minded artists like Leonardo da Vinci played a major role in revealing how distance is understood, through the techniques they used to portray distance in their paintings.

FIGURE 7. *The laws of perspective. An illustration in a 1505 treatise by Viator. (From W.M. Ivins (1975) 'On the Rationalization of Sight'. New York: Da Capo Press).*

What we do, apparently, is to use distance cues in 2-D images to interpret them in a 3-D way. There are two groups of distance cues:

monocular cues* (available to one eye).

binocular cues* (dependent upon the interaction of both eyes).

The monocular cues include a number of **pictorial** cues; these are properties of the image itself. **Non-pictorial** or physiological cues, on the other hand, are derived from the functioning of the eyes.

Monocular cues: pictorial

FIGURE 8. *The effect of relative size.*

1. Relative size

The further an object is from the eye, the smaller its image on the retina. As figure 8 illustrates, objects with smaller images may be seen as more distant. This phenomenon works especially well if you know the true sizes of the objects.

2. Relative brightness

Objects with brighter, clearer images are perceived as closer. You may have experienced this yourself if you have been up a tower or on a hilltop. The distant objects appear hazy whereas objects closer to you stand out more clearly. This phenomenon is also known as aerial perspective.

3. Superimposition

If the image of one object blocks the image of another object, the first object is seen as closer to you.

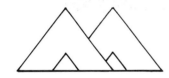

FIGURE 9. *Superimposition as a visual cue.*

4. Height in the visual field

If the image of one object is higher in the visual field, it is perceived as further away. You can see this in figure 8.

5. Texture gradient

Imagine that you are standing on a surface such as a field or beach. The sand grains or blades of grass are fairly regular in size, and so the images on your retina of those further from you will be smaller than the images of nearer ones. In other words, as Figure 10 illustrates, there is a gradient in the sizes of images of these texture elements, and the gradient tells you that the surface is receding from you in depth.

FIGURE 10. *An example of texture gradient.*

6. Linear perspective

As well as aerial perspective, mentioned above, artists make especial use of linear perspective to create the impression of distance in their paintings. Linear perspective refers to the fact that the images of parallel lines receding into the distance converge. This feature, together with aerial perspective, can be clearly seen in the illustration below, where the edges of the bridge appear to converge and the trees further away appear less distinct.

FIGURE 11. *Linear and aerial perspective.*

7. Motion parallax*

As an observer moves, images of more distant objects travel across the retina more slowly than images of nearer objects.

Monocular cue: non-pictorial

The only non-pictorial cue available to monocular vision is accommodation.

8. Accommodation

Think back to the structure of the eye explained at the beginning of this Unit and you will remember that the lens in your eye can change shape, or accommodate. This is necessary to keep the image of an object on the retina in sharp focus as it comes closer to the eye. The amount of accommodation of the lens is signalled to the brain and can be used as a guide to distance. This process provides depth cues to the brain up to a distance of about four feet.

The preceding eight cues are all available to binocular vision. In addition, there are two others that are exclusive to binocular vision since they depend on the processing of information from two eyes and their relative positions.

11

Binocular cues

1. Retinal disparity*

Because the eyes are about 6cms apart the retinas receive slightly different images. It is the superimposition of these two images that gives us stereoscopic vision.

If you have ever seen a 3-D film you will have been required to wear stereoscopic glasses which create the three-dimensional effect. Without the special glasses you would have seen two similar overlapping images taken from slightly different perspectives. The stereoscopic glasses ensure that one of these overlapping images is sent to your left eye and one to your right eye, just as though you were actually viewing a three-dimensional scene.

 SOMETHING TO TRY

Close one eye and line up a pen/pencil with a corner of the room. Now close that eye and open the other one and the pencil will appear to have moved. This is the result of the different images your eyes receive.

---

2. Convergence*

This cue also results from the fact that our eyes are several centimetres apart.

If you look at a distant object (more than 25 feet away) the line of vision to your two eyes is almost parallel, but the closer the object, the more your eyes have to turn inwards, towards the object.

If the object gets too close your eyes will not be able to converge anymore and you will experience double vision.

 Can you explain how a cat with one eye could survive and yet not be as efficient in catching its prey as a cat with two eyes?

As there are cues to inform depth perception which are essentially biological, and cues which would appear to be the result of our experience of the world, it is not surprising that psychologists have tried to determine whether perceptual ability is innate or learned. This issue will be considered in more detail in Part 4 of this Unit.

 A POSSIBLE PROJECT

Can you think of a way of testing the superiority of binocular vision over monocular vision? Here is one suggestion, for which you will need a needle, some Blu-tack, a long strip of paper marked every centimetre up to 50cms, and a pointer (a compass or a pencil would do).

Position your needle at the 45cm mark, using the Blu-tack to secure it. Place the paper at the edge of a table or desk and ask your participants to sit, in turn, so that they can just see the top of the pin over the edge of the table (see Figure 12).

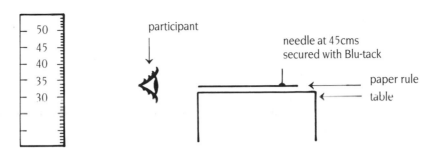

FIGURE 12. *The centimetre paper rule and the experimental set-up.*

Now ask each participant to cover both eyes and then move the pin to 35 and 40 cm positions. You will need to randomize the order of the presentations of the pin's distance. Ask your volunteer to open one or both eyes (again use some system of randomization) and to tell you (the investigator) to stop when the pointer appears to be level with the pin. Mark the resulting position down on a score sheet. You will end up with four results from each participant, similar to the following:

Target	Score
35 cm monocular vision (MV)	38 cm
35 cm binocular vision (BV)	34 cm
40 cm monocular vision (MV)	48 cm
40 cm binocular vision (BV)	40 cm

In each case, work out the difference between the distance of the pointer and the distance of the pin. These differences, or error scores, can then be averaged for each of the two conditions (MV and BV). (See your tutor if you need help with the statistics for this practical).

It is a very satisfying experiment to undertake, as you will always get significant results showing that binocular vision is superior.

SAQ
4

Why are two eyes more accurate, in terms of distance perception, than one?

Motion Perception

Is the perception of movement just a sequence of static sensations, that is, sensing an object in one location, and then sensing it in another?

One of the leading Gestalt psychologists, Wertheimer (1912), used a stroboscope to show this is not the case. Stroboscopic motion is produced when you flash a light in the darkness and a few milliseconds later you flash another light nearby. The perception will be of a single light moving from one spot to another as if in continuous motion. If the interval between the flashes is made too long, they are seen simply as two separate flashes of light in different places. The perception of motion is therefore a distinct experience, different from the perception of two stimuli, one after the other.

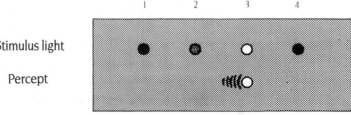

FIGURE 13. *Stroboscopic motion.*

The motion you see on the television screen or at the cinema is stroboscopic motion: each film is made up of thousands of static flashes. An animated cartoon is constructed from a sequence of drawings seen in quick succession.

Of course you more often perceive real motion. You have probably seen a train moving against the background of the countryside or town buildings. This **relative motion** is much easier to perceive than, say, the light of a plane against a pitch black night sky, where the **absolute motion** (against very few background cues) is much more difficult to detect.

When we detect relative motion, we sometimes experience an illusory perception of what is moving and what is stationary. Look at the moon on a cloudy, windy night. The moon appears to be moving through the clouds. This is an example of **induced motion**, and the explanation is that we unconsciously assume that the background (the clouds) must be stationary while the object apparently in the foreground (the moon) must be moving. In most situations, this assumption would be correct, but here it is wrong. You have experienced a similar illusion if you have sat in a stationary train and felt that you were moving when the train next to yours pulled out of the station.

Theories of perceptual organization

It should be becoming clear to you that perception is not in any way a random process, but rather it involves processing at both retinal and brain levels to make sense of the input. There are some basic principles which appear to govern this process.

Figure 14 can be hard to interpret (if you have not seen it before). Can you make sense of it?

It is, of course, a dalmation dog, but it is hard to detect because the **figure** (the dog) is indistinct from the **background**. We can never make sense of any object until we can see it as a coherent object and separate it from its background.

The Gestalt* psychologists, such as Koffka and Köhler, were particularly interested in the way in which visual perception is organized. (The German word 'Gestalt' means 'form').

According to these psychologists, 'the whole is greater than the sum of its parts'. When you try to analyse a stimulus into its constituent parts, there is a tendency to destroy the stimulus. Think of a painting. It is made up of a collection of daubs of paint, but the total impression is of a coherent whole.

FIGURE 14. *Figure-ground* problem.* (*After Street,* 1931. *Teachers College* Press).

Their fundamental principle of perceptual organization* was the Law of Prägnanz*, which was described by Koffka (1935) thus:

> *Of several geometrically possible organizations that one will actually occur which possesses the best, simplest and most stable shape.*

The Gestaltists formulated several laws which can be subsumed under the law of Prägnanz. Four of these laws are illustrated in Figures 15-18.

Proximity

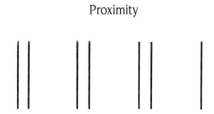

FIGURE 15. *The law of proximity: elements of a stimulus will be perceived as belonging together if they appear to be close together.*

Closure

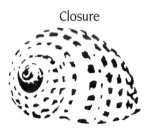

FIGURE 16. *The law of closure: an open or incomplete stimulus tends automatically to be perceived as closed because this makes the figure simpler to perceive.*

Good continuation

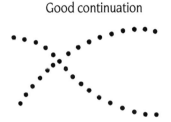

FIGURE 17. *The law of good continuation: we group together those elements requiring the fewest changes or interruptions in straight or curving lines.*

Similarity

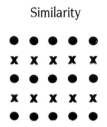

FIGURE 18. *The law of similarity: like or similar things are perceived together as part of the same pattern.*

If a stimulus has two or more distinct regions, you will perceive part of it as the figure (i.e. as more substantial) and the other as the ground (i.e. the background). Occasionally figure and ground are reversible and shifting depending on the context in which it is presented. For example, is Figure 19 a vase or two profiles?

FIGURE 19. *Rubin's Vase: a 'reversible' figure.*

Figure-ground reversal and art. Victor Vasarely. © DACS 1991.

The answer is, of course, that it is both! A less common example is Vasarely's print of two lovers embracing.

Evaluation of Gestalt principles

The Gestalt principles reflect sensible assumptions that a visual system can make about the world of objects. The problem of grouping together the elements in an image which belong together as parts of one object can be made easier by taking into account some simple facts.

(a) Elements close together are likely to be part of one object because matter is naturally cohesive (Figure 15).

(b) Interruptions in simple shapes, lines and curves are likely to be caused by nearer objects obscuring further ones (Figure 9).

(c) Similar elements are likely to belong together because the surfaces of natural objects have regular textures (Figure 18).

Although we can make drawings in which the grouping of elements into objects is ambiguous (Figures 14 and 19), such problems rarely occur in our perception of natural objects.

The Gestalt laws do give insights into the assumptions about the world upon which our visual perception is based, but they do not tell us how the brain processes information from the retinal image to organize it into separate objects. Some light has been thrown on this problem by experiments which demonstrate that the overall forms of patterns are analysed *before* the detailed elements of which they are made up. Navon (1977) used patterns in which small letters were arranged so as to make up the shapes of larger letters, as illustrated in Figure 20.

```
   H H H
 H       H
 H
 H
   H H H
       H
           H
 H         H
   H H H H
```

FIGURE 20. An *example of the part-whole relationship.*

When people were asked to identify the large letter (the 'S' in Figure 20), they were not influenced by the identity of the smaller letters making it up (the H's). On the other hand, they were sometimes influenced by the large one when asked to identify the smaller ones. This result tells us that identification of the global pattern of a stimulus like this can be achieved without having to first identify its constituent features; the 'whole' can be seen before the 'parts', as Gestalt psychology would have argued.

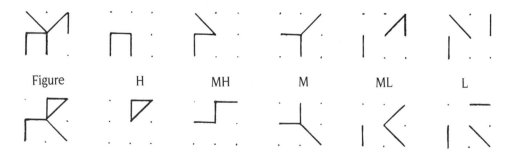

| Figure | H | MH | M | ML | L |

FIGURE 21. One of Palmer's 6 segment figures (left) with possible 3 segments parts classified as high (H), medium high (MH), medium (M), medium low (ML) and low (L) likelihood in terms of perceptual organization. (From Palmer (1977), **Cognitive Psychology**, 9, p 452).

Similarly, Palmer (1977) showed that analysis of a visual form takes place hierarchically, starting with the overall configuration and moving down to its basic elements. Participants were asked to divide six-segment figures into three-segment parts (see Figure 21). Preferences for groupings were consistent and supported the idea that perceptual processing is hierarchical.

Marr (1982) showed how the Gestalt principles could be used in a visual processing program, to reveal important structures hidden within the mass of data which comprises the natural images available to us.

Perceptual constancies

In order to understand fully the process of perception it is necessary to examine those occasions when there is a discrepancy between reality and what is perceived. This can occur as a result of perceptual constancy*, ambiguity or illusion*.

Whenever we look at an object, such as a tree (the distal stimulus*) we don't in fact get our information about that tree from the object itself, but rather from the retinal image of the tree (the proximal stimulus*). The perceptual system interprets a wide variety of different proximal stimulus patterns as one object.

Shape constancy

Look at a closed door. It is rectangular in shape. Open it a little and it still appears rectangular, even though the image which falls on the retina will be trapezoid. This is an example of shape constancy which occurs when an object's shape is perceived as constant irrespective of the angle from which it is viewed.

FIGURE 22. *Shape constancy: a door viewed at various open positions.*

Size constancy

Despite the fact that the retinal image of an object 50 feet away is twice the size of the retinal image of the same object 100 feet away, we still understand that the object has not grown or shrunk. This is the result of size constancy.

A POSSIBLE PROJECT

You can design an experiment to test size constancy using a series of cardboard boxes covered (or painted) similarly, but with different letters marked on them. Your participants are asked to tell you which boxes are larger, smaller or the same size. Compare their ability to do this in two situations; one where the boxes are placed near objects which provide plenty of depth information, and one where the boxes are placed on a large open surface such as a playing field with no nearby objects. You could use the same field in both cases, putting the boxes near buildings or trees at its edges in the first case, and in the centre in the second case. If participants are able to estimate sizes more accurately in the first case, then you will have found out that depth cues from surrounding objects contribute to size constancy. You will probably also need to blindfold participants between trials so they are unable to see you moving boxes from one position to another.

Lightness constancy

We are capable of perceiving the lightness of an object regardless of rather drastic changes in the illumination that may fall upon it. This is termed lightness constancy. A swan swimming on a lake does not suddenly turn grey because a storm cloud blocks the sun; it appears just as white, merely in shadow. It probably works because when illumination changes, it affects not only the object in the foreground, but also the background against which it is seen. The result is that the brain automatically compensates.

SOMETHING TO TRY

You can investigate lightness constancy and the impact of background cues by viewing a range of objects through a cardboard tube (the inside of a long kitchen roll) in a number of different light conditions. The tube allows you to focus on single objects and eliminates background.

Colour constancy

Colour constancy also refers to an ability to maintain a constant perception despite changes in lighting. Imagine that you are looking at a white surface such as a sheet of paper in daylight. If you take it indoors, under artificial light, it will reflect more red light and less blue light than it did outdoors, because sunlight and artificial light contain different proportions of these wavelengths. Despite the change in the colour of light reflected from the paper, the colour you perceive does not change — it looks white, and not reddish-orange. Colour constancy is not perfect as you may have discovered if you have ever bought an item of clothing from a shop under fluorescent lighting and then found the colours appear different under normal lighting.

SOMETHING TO TRY

Using several long cardboard tubes with coloured transparent paper (such as sweet wrappings) secured over the ends you can examine the effects of the different coloured filters on a series of coloured squares. Are colour changes more marked when the squares are viewed singly, as opposed to in combination with each other? Why do you think this is?

Location constancy

In normal vision, our eyes move many times each second. Each time, the image of an object will move over the retina just as if the object itself moved. Any movement of our head or body will also cause the image to move over the retina. Yet we are able to interpret this motion as arising from our own movement, and to perceive the object as remaining stationary. This ability is called location constancy, and there are a number of theories which attempt to explain it. One possibility is that we interpret motion of the whole image as the result of our own movement, but motion of part of it as the result of movement of an object. Another is that the brain uses information about eye, head and body movements to calculate what motion of the image would be expected if nothing around us was moving, and we see any difference as object motion. It is quite likely that both these mechanisms work together.

SAQ 5

James (1890) described a baby's world as one of 'blooming, buzzing confusion'. Suggest at least five laws of organization that help people to make sense of the world.

Perceptual Illusions

What can ambiguity and illusion tell us about normal perception? First of all we must understand what perceptual illusions are.

An illusion is a distorted, or false, percept. If you were to use some kind of measuring device you would be able to prove that the actual situation was different from the perceived situation. Gregory (1966) identified four kinds of visual illusions.

1. Geometric Illusions

In geometric illusions some aspect of a line drawing appears distorted and we are likely to make a wrong judgement. Probably the most well known is the Müller-Lyer illusion illustrated in Figure 23. Which line is the longer of the two?

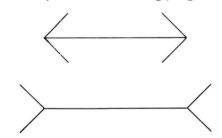

FIGURE 23. *The Müller-Lyer illusion.*

You probably perceive the bottom line as longer. This is because the outward-spreading fins mislead you. In fact, if you were to measure the two lines, you would find that they are identical in length.

Figure 24 is the Ponzo illusion. You have to decide if one of the two horizontal lines is longer than the other. The answer, once again, is that they are both the same length.

Here the illusion stems from the fact that the stimulus resembles a three-dimensional scene, as the converging lines provide the cue of linear perspective (see page 11). The brain processes the image in this way as though it were three-dimensional, so the top line appears longer.

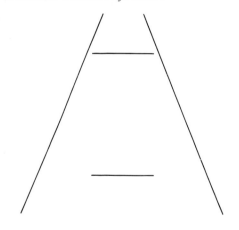

FIGURE 24. *The Ponzo illusion.*

In the circles illusion, the central circle in the left hand figure appears smaller than in the right hand figure, despite the fact that they are identical in size.

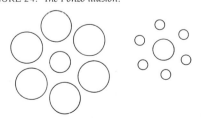

FIGURE 25. *The circles illusion.*

19

2. Ambiguous Figures

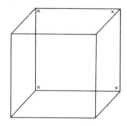

FIGURE 26. *The Necker Cube.*

A well known ambiguous figure* is the Necker Cube. If you concentrate on the side with the crosses, it can either be the rear side of the cube, or the top side (looking down).

You may well find yourself experiencing the uncomfortable sensation of the two views changing rapidly from one to the other as you look at this illusion.

3. Paradoxical Figures

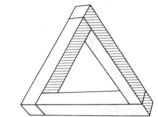

FIGURE 27. A *paradoxical figure —*
the Penrose Impossible Triangle.

In the case of paradoxical figures we make false assumptions about them. In the Penrose Impossible Triangle these assumptions are about the distance the three corners are away from us.

4. Fictions

The last group of illusions are called the fictions because we see something which is actually not there. In Figure 28, it is a triangle that we can see.

FIGURE 28. *The Kanizsa Triangle.*

What does the study of perceptual illusions show us about normal perception? Because ambiguous stimuli can be perceived in more than one way, but only one percept is experienced at a time, then a selective process must also be part of perception.

Gregory has suggested that we are misled by a geometric illusion because we read depth and distance cues into the two-dimensional images. He explains the Müller-Lyer illusion in terms of our understanding of perspective cues.

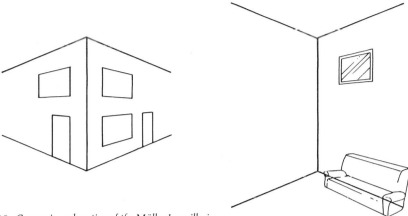

FIGURE 29. *Gregory's explanation of the Müller-Lyer illusion.*

The ingoing fins resemble the corners closest to us, of a building, whereas the outgoing fins resemble the walls of a room which we are in. The retinal images of both are in fact equal, but our brain, in trying to make a sensible interpretation of the data present, employs size constancy. This leads us to believe that the line which is interpreted as further away, must be longer.

Stacey and Pike (1970) have challenged Gregory's explanation, arguing that apparent size determines distance rather than the reverse. It should also be noted that the Müller-Lyer effect works even when the fins are replaced by other attachments such as circles or squares, as in Figure 30.

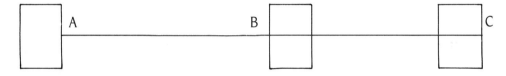

FIGURE 30. *A variation on the Müller-Lyer illusion — the distance between A and B is the same as the distance between B and C.*

Impossible figures tell us something about how pictorial cues in a line drawing are integrated to achieve an impression of depth. If an impossible figure is drawn small enough that its image lies within the fovea, it appears to be flat, and lacks any impression of solidity (Hochberg, 1978). This suggests that, in integrating depth cues from a line drawing, we do not combine together the information we obtain from successive glances at different parts of it. If we did, then an impossible figure such as Figure 27 would also appear flat. Hochberg argues that we do not need to integrate depth information from one glance to another, as the real objects we see in the natural world always have a consistent solid structure.

Using the explanation for the Müller-Lyer illusion as a clue, can you think of a possible explanation for the Ponzo illusion?

A POSSIBLE PROJECT

According to a number of explanations for the Müller-Lyer illusion (including Gregory's), the angle of the fins ought to be a relevant feature. Try the illusion out on a number of participants with three different fin angles, such as 30°, 45° and 60°. What explanations can you suggest for your results?

Object Recognition

KEY AIMS: By the end of this section you will:

▷ *have an understanding of patttern recognition theories*

▷ *have been introduced to Marr's Computational Theory*

▷ *understand the influences which determine what we do or don't perceive in any given situation*

▷ *appreciate the difference between bottom-up and top-down processing systems.*

Pattern recognition theories

What do the shapes below have in common?

B **B** B *B* B *B*

Of course they are all examples of the letter 'B' in various sizes, typeface styles and handwritten forms. The ability to recognize a multiplicity of pattern forms as the same item is a very impressive aspect of visual perception. It is obvious that in order to achieve this feat some kind of pattern-recognition must take place. This has had particular importance in the automatic reading of postcodes. The business community uses many printers capable of producing the letter 'B' in a variety of different ways, added to which we also write the letter 'B' in an equally wide range of ways. An automatic postcode reader then has a tricky job to recognize exactly which range of shapes to accept as a letter 'B'.

The Kurzweil Personal Reader, a computerized scanner, has enabled many blind people to 'read' their mail, documents and other type-written material, for the first time. This breakthrough using computer technology is an example of how it may be possible to build artificial systems which can simulate complex human psychological processes. The Personal Reader is able to distinguish letters of the alphabet no matter what style they are printed in.

Three theoretical approaches to pattern recognition have been proposed and each of them is explained briefly.

1. Template theory*

According to this theory we have a number of templates (or miniature copies) of previously experienced patterns held in permanent memory. A new stimulus is compared to a template to produce the closest match.

This theory is quite attractive at first sight, until you consider the number of templates that would have to be in permanent store to allow for all changes in size, orientation, etc. Of course, it is possible that any input goes through some kind of normalization process to reduce it to a standard size and orientation, but it still fails to explain how we can recognize new stimuli as belonging to a loosely defined category such as 'buildings' — no one template would ever be adequate.

2. Prototype theory

Prototype theory* argues that every member of a particular class shares certain key attributes. For example, a prototypical table might consist of four legs supporting a flat surface. Each 'table-like' stimulus encountered would then be compared with the prototype and accepted or rejected.

One big advantage of this approach over template theory is that there would be a lower (although still very substantial) number of prototypes stored in memory, rather than an enormous number of templates. The weakness of this approach lies in the fact that it does not explain the details of the matching process. It also fails to explain how context can affect pattern recognition.

3. Feature theory

This approach attempts to overcome the limitations of the two previous theories. It assumes that any pattern consists of a set of specific features or attributes. These features are extracted from the present stimulus and then combined and compared with a bank of such features stored in permanent memory. This reduces the number of features that can be combined and recombined to allow for pattern recognition.

Feature detection theory* receives some support from studies of the responses of single cells in the brain. The Nobel prizewinners, Hubel and Wiesel (1979), found that certain cells in the visual cortex (the first major part of the brain to receive visual information) are responsive to lines and edges at particular angles. The technique which led to this discovery involves anaesthetizing an animal and placing it in a device which holds its head in a fixed position. Patterns of light are then projected onto a screen in front of the animal so that their images fall on particular parts of the retina. A microelectrode is implanted near a single neuron in the visual cortex of the animal and the activity in the neuron caused by the light stimulus can be seen on an oscilloscope and recorded.

Hubel and Wiesel proposed that the cells in the visual system of the brain are arranged as a hierarchy of feature detectors*. At the lowest level are simple cells, which respond to a line of a particular orientation at a particular place on the retina. These simple cells then feed information to complex cells, which respond to the same kind of stimulus anywhere within the retina. These in turn pass information on to hypercomplex cells, which respond to edges ending in a particular area, and so might detect corners.

It is tempting to think that we might find higher and higher levels of this hierarchy, especially when we see results like those of Perrett et al. (1988), who found cells in the brains of monkeys which respond to the faces of particular monkeys or people. However, the theory that cats, monkeys and people have one cell in the brain for each kind of thing they need to recognize is highly controversial, and all these results can also be explained by the theory that visual recognition of a familiar pattern, object or person depends on the activity of large networks of brain cells.

The feature theory of pattern recognition is not as clearly supported by research on the brain as was once thought. Although it can cope with some psychological findings on pattern recognition (Neisser 1967; Lindsay and Norman, 1972), there are others it cannot explain. In particular, it underemphasizes the roles of context and expectations.

23

Marr's Computational Theory (1982)

With the advances in artificial intelligence* in the 1970s, it was hoped that it would soon be possible to design machines that would be able to recognize objects in the real world. Once researchers started working in this area they quickly realized how complex a task is visual perception. To understand it requires a blending of our knowledge of both the physiology and the psychology of visual perception as well as a knowledge of artificial intelligence.

According to Marr, seeing requires a sequence of representations, each one derived from its predecessor by an appropriate set of processes. The task of visual processing is to create a description of the object viewed from the image which is presented.

In viewing any scene we begin with an image from which we obtain a 'grey level description' which tells us of the intensity at each point (pixel) in the image. From this we develop a 'primal sketch' which provides important information about the two-dimensional image including the intensity changes, their geometric distribution and organization. The next stage in visual processing is the '2.5-D sketch' which provides information on the orientation, rough depth and motion of objects and surfaces. The final level is the '3-D object description' which details shapes and their spatial organization. This is the stage where recognition takes place.

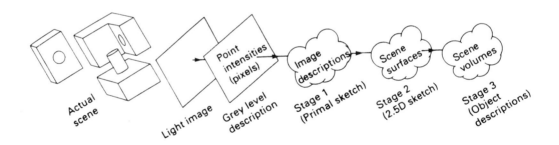

FIGURE 31. *Marr's major stages of representation.* (From I. Roth and J. Frisby (1986) **Perception and Representation**. *Open University Press.*)

Marr's theory of visual perception is unique in recognizing that its starting point should be an understanding of the functions of visual perception and the nature of the information in images of natural scenes that could be used to achieve these functions. He asked **what** an observer needs to compute from the pattern of light on the retina, and **why**, before going on to develop his theory of **how** this information could be computed. The value of the approach can be seen by the analogy to studying a bird's feather in the hope of understanding the process of flight. It is clearly insufficient to examine the feather in isolation, because something must be known of aerodynamics also. Similarly, to study visual perception by examining the biological basis, neurons, or the psychological factors in isolation, is doomed to failure, but rather we should be looking at the nature of the visual task itself that is being solved by the visual system. This was Marr's contribution to the area — to analyse the **function** of visual perception.

Outline and evaluate three theories of perceptual organization.

Perceptual set

At any one time what we perceive is a function of perceptual set. Allport (1955) defined perceptual set as 'a perceptual bias or predisposition or readiness to perceive particular features of a stimulus'. In other words, set is operating when you notice some features of a stimulus and ignore others.

EG: *When you are waiting to cross a road, you notice where and how fast the vehicles are moving on the road. You are less likely to notice many details of the person standing right next to you.*

A number of factors influence perceptual set. Although they have been arranged to form a mnemonic, MICE CREED, they should not be thought of as independent of each other.

- — **M** motivation
- — **I** instructions
- — **C** context
-    **E** expectations
- — **C** cultural factors
- — **R** reward and punishment
- — **E** emotion
- — **E** (past) experience
- — **D** (individual) differences

Motivation

Motivation has a direct influence on perceptual set. Gilchrist and Nesberg (1952) found that hungry and thirsty people perceived pictures of food and drink as being brighter than pictures of other objects. Estimates of the brightness of the pictures fell to the base levels recorded at the start of the experiment once participants were allowed to eat and drink.

Instructions

Prior instructions can influence perceptual set.

SOMETHING TO TRY

Using Figure 32, try the illustration on three different people. Ask the first person to think of an old professor before looking at the picture. Ask the second to think of an animal and ask the third person to report what they see, without any prior instructions.

What results did you get?

You probably found that the instructions predisposed your participants to perceive something related to your instructions. Your third participant probably reported seeing a mouse or a rat, because there are more depth cues to support that interpretation, whereas the picture interpreted as a 'professor' is relatively flat.

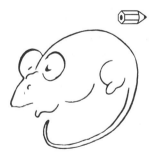

FIGURE 32. *Stimulus to show the effect of instructions.*

Context

This refers to anything that might help you to identify the stimulus (apart from the stimulus itself).

Figures 33 (a) and (b) show how influential the context can be over our perceptions. The middle stimulus of the two sequences is ambiguous, but in the left sequence it is perceived as a 'B', and in the right sequence it is perceived as a '13'. The only difference is in the other contextual cues.

FIGURE 33   (a)   (b)

The sequence of pictures in Figure 34 show a young woman.

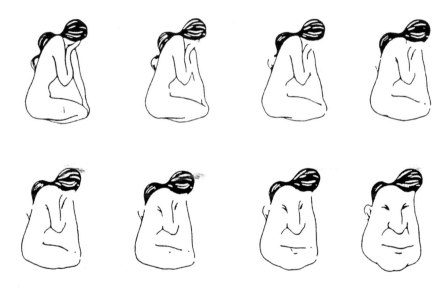

FIGURE 34. *Temporal context effects.*

Once you reach the middle of the sequence the pictures are ambiguous. If you were to start looking at the sequence from the other end, you would perceive distorted faces. This is known as the temporal context effect.

If a stimulus appears in an unusual context recognition tends to be slower. Imagine how hard it would be to recognize the soberly dressed librarian you see daily when she is dressed in skin tight leather clothes singing with a rock band.

Expectations

Expectations can help us to find a stimulus much faster. Marcel (1983) flashed the word 'bread' on to a screen for a few milliseconds and then the word 'butter'. Participants recognized 'butter' more quickly having been exposed to the word 'bread', then they would if no such exposure took place.

You have probably experienced this helpful aspect of perceptual set when meeting someone from a train, or in a crowded shopping area. You can pick them out of the crowd easily because you are expecting to see them. It would be more difficult to pick them out of a similar-sized crowd where you didn't expect to meet them.

Cultural factors

This is increasingly difficult to observe nowadays with mass communications, since few groups are culturally isolated from the rest of the world.

Turnbull (1961) reports on the Bambuti pygmies living in the rain forests of the Congo. When a pygmy was taken to an open plain where buffalo were grazing in the distance, he thought they were insects, and as the insects 'grew' into buffalo as they were approached by vehicle, he accused Turnbull of witchcraft. This is an example of the pygmy lacking size constancy over large distances (although presumably not smaller ones).

Reward and punishment

Schafer and Murphy (1974) used the pictures of two juxtaposed faces (Figure 35) to show how reward and punishment could influence perceptual set.

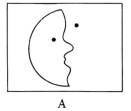 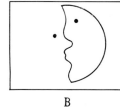 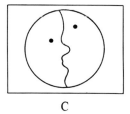

| A | B | C |

FIGURE 35. *Stimulus used to demonstrate the effects of reward and punishment.*

Whenever 'A' was shown the participant was rewarded with money, but the money was withdrawn (punishment) when 'B' was shown. Participants were asked to learn to name the faces. When 'C' was shown it was more often reported to be 'A' than 'B'.

Emotion

McGinnies (1949) flashed sexual, taboo and neutral words in front of people while recording their psycho-galvanic skin responses* (which indicate level of physiological arousal). Half the participants were slower to perceive the taboo words, but their arousal levels were far higher than for neutral words. This investigation also supports the idea that words can be recognized before they reach consciousness, since participants must have detected that there was something different about the taboo words before they were consciously aware of them.

Experience

The effect of past experience was demonstrated by Bruner and Goodman (1947). They asked ten-year-olds to alter a spot of light until it matched the size of a coin in another part of the visual field. In most cases, children over-estimated the size of the coin, roughly in line with the coin's value (i.e. the greater over-estimates were for the coins of higher value).

Bruner and Goodman found that children from poorer homes over-estimated the size of the coins to a greater degree than children from more privileged homes. Other researchers have suggested that this could be due to lack of familiarity with the coins and their true sizes.

Individual differences

Witkin et al. (1954) identified two different perceptual types: field dependent* and field independent* people. The field dependent person is more likely to be influenced by distracting or irrelevant features when attempting to perceive objects than is the field independent person.

Witkin developed the Embedded Figures Test to indicate whether individuals are field dependent or independent. In this test, as the name suggests, the person is asked to find a particular stimulus among distracting visual stimuli.

According to Witkin, domineering, rule-bound parents are likely to encourage field dependence in their children by their attention to and control of contexts of behaviour, whereas less rule-orientated parents encourage field independence. There was also a sex difference, with males being more likely to be field independent, although this may be the result of the different ways parents raise boys and girls rather than an innate sex difference.

Identify five different biases which result in a person noticing some features of a stimulus, while ignoring others.

Can you think of any evolutionary, or other reason, why human perceptual ability might be biased by perceptual set?

Bottom-up and top-down processing systems

The factors discussed in the previous section illustrate what are known as 'top-down'* influences on perception; what we see is affected by higher level factors such as our emotions or knowledge as well as by the lower level characteristics of the stimulus itself. The pattern recognition theories described earlier have a different emphasis; they try to explain how patterns and objects could be recognized on the basis of stimulus characteristics alone, through 'bottom-up'* processing. Marr was especially concerned in his theory to discover how much can be achieved in perception through bottom-up processing. He showed that it is possible, for example, to segment an image of a scene into objects without necessarily knowing what the shapes and sizes in it are. Even so, we know that bottom-up processing of visual information is sometimes inadequate and that top-down processes must play a role.

In some situations, we do need to know from experience the sizes of objects in order to see their size correctly. The vertical-horizontal illusion (Figure 36) shows that we tend to overestimate the length of vertical lines, and the illusion occurs even when we substitute everyday items such as spoons for drawn lines. Another common perceptual error is to perceive large distant objects as smaller than they really are.

FIGURE 36. *The vertical-horizontal illusion.*

Bruner (1957) and Gregory (1972) place a particularly strong emphasis on top-down or conceptually-driven processing. They view perception as an active, constructive process, not one driven by the stimulus input, but one which is the end-product of the interaction between the context of the stimulus and perceiver expectations. Gregory's explanation for the Müller-Lyer illusion as being the result of experience of perspective (see page 21) is an example of top-down processing (although one which has subsequently been challenged, for example by Marr, 1976).

So, on what does visual perception depend: bottom-up or top-down processing?

Perception clearly involves the interaction between both top-down and bottom-up processing. For example, a perceiver's expectations may be initially very vague and general, but become progressively more specific as more stimulus information becomes available. Similarly, expectations, as we have already seen in this Unit, play an important part in determining which attributes of a stimulus will receive attention.

The balance between the relative importance of top-down and bottom-up processing does seem to be changed by viewing conditions. In natural conditions the world provides a rich source of visual information, which we have time to sample and explore actively. As a result, there is often enough information available for bottom-up processing to provide an accurate description of our surroundings. If viewing conditions are restricted in some way, then we often become more dependent on top-down processing. This happens if stimuli are presented very briefly (tachistoscopically), so that we haven't enough time to scan them, or if they are simplified line drawings without texture and depth cues. In such circumstances, bottom-up processing may give incomplete results, and we have to make guesses about a stimulus based on our knowledge and expectations.

Development of Perception

KEY AIMS: By the end of this section you will:

▷ *appreciate the nature-nurture debate as it applies to perception*

▷ *understand the relevance of deprivation studies to this argument*

▷ *have an insight into how faces are perceived.*

As with many areas of psychology there is an ongoing debate about where the ability to perceive comes from. The early thinkers divided up into two camps: the empiricists*, who believed that all human ability is the result of experience, and the nativists*, who argued that everything was innately given.

The Empiricist Position

An early empiricist philosopher was John Locke (1632-1704). He argued that at birth a child's mind is a blank sheet, a tabula rasa, on which every experience leaves its mark. Locke's position was particularly well-received at the time when Europe had little time for the landed gentry and the so-called divine right of kings. Many people welcomed the idea that all people were essentially equal, the only difference being due to environmental influences.

The empiricists then, held that prior experience was what shaped our ability to make sense of the world. They believed association* to be the key to this. Association is the process by which one sensation is linked to another. This is basically a very simple idea: that if two sensations occur together often enough, eventually one of them will evoke the idea of the other one.

The Nativist Position

The roots of nativism go back to the Greek philosopher Plato. Nativists assert that much of our perceptual ability is the result of our natural endowment and does not depend upon learning. One influential philosopher of the nativist perspective was Immanuel Kant (1724-1804).

Kant argued that our knowledge of the world could not come from sensory information alone, but that there had to be certain pre-existing 'categories' to order and organize the sensory data. Examples of these categories are space, time and causality. Kant believed that these were built into the mind a priori (i.e. as basic working principles). According to Kant there was no way you could see the world except in terms of these categories. Imagine that you were born wearing rose-tinted spectacles, then everything in your experience would be coloured pink by those glasses. This is what happens, according to Kant, with the a priori categories. They order and organize all sensory information experienced by a person, but they are innately determined.

Outline in the simplest possible way the nativist and empiricist positions.

The nature/nurture debate

It has become clear that neither position can be supported in its purest form, but what is interesting to determine is the relative contribution of nature* (the nativist perspective) and nurture* (the empiricist position) — the extent to which perception is the result of learning, and how that learning is achieved. Researchers have tried in many ways to isolate the effects of inheritance from experience in order to determine just how much of our perceptual ability is present from birth.

Deprivation studies

Although there is some initial retinal processing, most of the more advanced processing goes on in the brain. At the simplest level, the brain has detector cells that respond to elementary features such as bars, lines and edges of objects. Evidence to support the empiricists' view of perception has come from various studies conducted upon cats and monkeys to investigate the impact of deprivation of visual stimuli on these detector cells.

Blakemore and Cooper (1970) reared kittens in environments where they were only exposed to vertical stripes or to horizontal stripes. After five months of this, the kittens were blind to objects in the orientation which had been denied to them. What this meant in practice was that a kitten reared with access only to horizontal stripes would not then respond to a piece of string dangled in front of it. Anyone with a cat of their own will find this hard to imagine! What it meant for the psychologist was evidence that whatever cats (and by generalization, humans) are born with in the way of physiology was not sufficient to explain the process of perception, but experience in the form of exposure to stimulation, is essential to ensure the complete functioning of the visual system.

That this might also be the case for humans had been suggested by Senden (1960), although his results were not as clear-cut as the later animal work. Senden looked at individuals who had been blind from birth with cataracts on both eyes and who subsequently had their vision restored to them after operations when they were adults.

The patients were able to fixate and scan images, follow a moving finger with their eyes and distinguish figure from ground. These abilities, then, appear to be innate. However, the patients had difficulty identifying by sight objects such as cutlery or faces which were already familiar to them by touch. They needed to count the corners before they could distinguish a square from a triangle. It took several weeks of training before the patients could identify these simple objects by sight.

What this work shows is that some visual capacity exists even in people who have had no visual experience. There are difficulties with adult-restored vision, however, since we can never know if any part of the visual system has deteriorated after years of disuse. Also, despite having been blind, these adults will have amassed a great deal of information about the world which allows them to take maximum advantage of any information their visual system does pick up and, as has already been implied, they learn to rely on other senses. It is, therefore, not possible to make any generalizations about a new-born baby's visual ability by comparison with adults' restored vision.

Evidence for innate mechanisms

Fantz (1956) developed the 'preference technique' to discover what babies looked at. This involved showing two or more stimuli to infants. By studying the eye movements carefully, researchers have been able to work out the 'rules babies look by' (Haith, 1980). More recent work in this area has used more sophisticated equipment including heartbeat or brain wave monitors to record what happens when babies are presented with new stimuli.

Certainly, babies as young as six weeks scan their visual world systematically to find out where objects are (Salapatek, 1975). Later, they will scan each object in a systematic way so as to extract maximum information. This happens at about eight weeks of age and is associated with identifying objects more than merely detecting their presence or absence.

Gibson (1969) has identified four basic perceptual strategies which children tend to move through from infancy to adolescence.

1. **Capture to activity:** this describes a general shift from scanning the environment in the hope that something will capture the attention, to interest and intention becoming more important influences on what will be perceived.

2. **Less systematic to more systematic search:** strategies become more complex. Although a new object will be examined visually in a systematic way by a baby, as the child gets older recognition will be better because the child can draw on earlier visual, manual etc. examination.

3. **Broad to selective pick-up of information:** as children become older they are better able to focus on a single aspect of a complex situation.

4. **Ignoring irrelevant information:** this may seem the same as the previous point, but here it is not just a question of focusing in on one item, but rather to do with distractability. For example, in the exam room, you have to be able to shut out the squeaky chair, the sniffing student, the tutors walking up and down the rows and direct all your energies to the question paper.

Shape perception as an innate ability

Bower (1966) investigated shape constancy in 2-month-old babies using operant conditioning techniques. The babies were reinforced for turning their heads when they saw a particular shape, such as a rectangle. The shape was then tilted or turned in some way. Even though the retinal images were different from the original rectangular shape the babies still responded, thereby demonstrating at least some shape constancy. The ability may be present even earlier, but we have no information about this at present.

Depth perception as an innate ability

In an attempt to determine whether depth perception was learned or innate, Gibson and Walk (1960) used the 'visual cliff'*. This is a device with two surfaces made up of the same pattern, but covered with a sheet of thick glass. One surface is stepped down from the other by a couple of feet.

Gibson and Walk tested infants ranging from 6-14 months by placing them in the central area. Almost all infants crawled on to the shallow side, despite their mothers calling to them from the cliff side.

FIGURE 37. *The 'Visual Cliff' experiment. (By permission of William Vandivert and* **Scientific American**, 1960).

SAQ 10

Can you suggest why the 'visual cliff' experiment fails to prove that the ability to perceive depth is innate?

In order to counter criticisms concerning the Gibson and Walk experiment, other workers have tested chicks, lambs and goats as soon as they are capable of standing. The animals characteristically froze when placed on the deep side and always chose the shallow side when placed in the central area.

Face perception

Faces are particularly special to us. People play such an important part in all human beings' lives that it is not surprising that our ability to perceive faces has been investigated by many psychologists. In particular, they have tried to establish whether face perception is innate or learned. Goren et al. (1975) have shown that infants with a mean age of just nine minutes follow with their eyes a stimulus which resembles a schematic face, rather than a blank head shape or one with scrambled features.

Probably the best known worker in this area of perception is Fantz (1961) who first showed that human infants have a very early tendency to look at forms which resemble the human face, although it is likely that this is probably the result of a preference for the visual components which make up a face (such as curved lines).

33

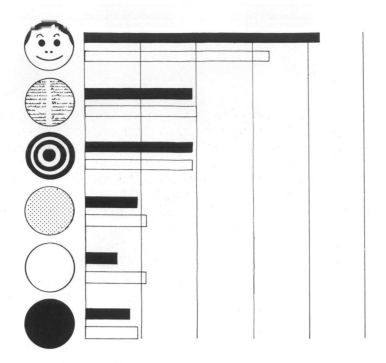

FIGURE 38. *The upper bar of each pair indicates looking time for 2- to 3-month-olds, the lower bar for babies of 4 months old. (From R.L. Fantz 1961).*

He demonstrated this by putting infants in his looking chamber and recording their gaze at a range of stimuli.

FIGURE 39. *Fantz's looking chamber.*

Later work has suggested that this preference is transitory (true face recognition requiring the maturation of cortical structures) and it is suggested that this early ability may help the bonding process between newborn and mother by encouraging mother to pay more attention to her new infant. This predisposition is obviously of great importance to human infants who have a very long period of dependency compared with other animals.

Over the first year of life, children become increasingly proficient at face recognition. According to Carey and Diamond (1977) younger children process information about faces in a rather piecemeal fashion, attending primarily to specific features. It is much later that they are able to attend to the configural information contained in the faces. This means that it is relatively easy to confuse young children (aged three to five) by wearing a hat or a particular expression, for example. This could also account for why children up to the age of about six accept different adults dressed in the costume of Santa Claus as Santa Claus.

A developmental dip in the ability to recognize faces has been reported by Diamond et al. (1983) which may be linked to the fact that prior to puberty there is no cerebral hemispheric asymmetry (i.e. the right hemisphere only becomes superior for face processing around puberty). Although the right hemisphere's superiority has been supported by a variety of workers in this area, it is also true to say that the left hemisphere has considerable ability, but may adopt different strategies (Sergent, 1982).

The condition prosopagnosia, which is the total inability to recognize faces, has also added to our knowledge of how face recognition takes place. Sufferers from this condition (the result of some form of brain damage) may be able to read and recognize everyday objects and yet not recognize family, friends or teachers. It is clear from this that the process of face perception may differ from other perceptual abilities. Currently, work is going on in the area of how normal face perception develops in the hope that this will provide greater understanding of adult face perception systems.

The process of face perception is believed to involve three stages.

1. The face is compared with a set of stored descriptions called face recognition units, and this culminates in a feeling of being familiar (or not) with the presented face.

2. Your memory store is activated to remember something about the person, such as what they do or where you last saw them.

3. The retrieval of the name from memory.

These stages will fit with your own experience, because you are likely to have had the experience of recognizing a face, even knowing that the individual is a television personality, but being unable to name them. It makes sense to assume that the name is stored in a separate area from the face recognition area because, in an evolutionary sense, the name is not so important as knowing whether it is a friend or foe.

These three stages are what is known as 'black boxes': that is we know what they do, but we don't know how they do it. Bruce (1989) suggests that we build up a kind of representation of how each face differs from the average and so we carry a kind of prototype face in our memory and this may give us some insight into how stage one works. Haig (1986) using computer images has shown that the most important feature in photograph recognition is the shape of the head, followed by the eyes and then the mouth. This work however, like much of the work in this area, has concentrated on full-face images. The nose is likely to be of greater importance in profile recognition.

Perception — innate or learned?

It would seem that the most sensible answer to this question is to make an analogy with computer software (the computer programs) and hardware (the computer itself). The 'hardware' of the perceptual system includes specific neural pathways and sensitive periods for the development of particular functions, and this may well be genetically pre-programmed. The 'software', however — the ability to function in the real world — depends on specific experiences.

There is no doubt that children are able to discriminate visually in the very early days of life, but more specific discriminations require specific experiences in order to build up a repertoire of separate objects, people and the like.

Summarize, with appropriate criticisms, the evidence for each side of the nature/nurture debate with regard to visual perception.

If any element of perceptual ability is learned, what implications does this have for carers of very young children?

Postscript

KEY AIMS: By the end of this section you will:

▷ *have been introduced to two controversial areas of the psychology of perception*

▷ *be aware of the limitations of the claims in these areas.*

Extra-sensory perception

Are we able to perceive things without using our basic five senses? This is the claim of ESP (extra-sensory perception*).

There are three varieties of ESP:

telepathy — sending, or perceiving, of thought from one person to another

clairvoyance — perceiving remote events

precognition — perceiving future events.

Linked with ESP claims are those of psychokinesis (PK) — the ability to move things by a process of mind over matter.

Most people's experience of ESP is based on staged performances, which are quite different from what the parapsychologist (those who study happenings which are beyond the normal) would be involved with in the controlled situation of the laboratory. In the stage performance, the psychic controls all that is seen and heard, whereas in the laboratory it is the experimenter who controls all that the psychic sees and hears. We should not, therefore, be surprised that laboratory investigations of even well-known psychics fail to live up to their promise.

Experimental evidence

Rhine (1942) did much of the early research in this area using a card guessing procedure. The typical ESP card pack consists of 25 cards with 5 different symbols, as shown in Figure 40. The advantages of the card-guessing procedure include:

(a) it can be carefully controlled;

(b) there is little possibility of cheating;

(c) the experiment can be repeated with the same person at different times, or with different people;

(d) the statistical significance of the outcome can be easily determined.

FIGURE 40. ESP *cards.*

By guesswork alone a person should score, on average, 5 successful hits. Even very successful participants rarely score as many as seven hits on a regular basis (although their scores may be statistically significant).

The arguments against the existence of ESP and PK (psychokinesis) can be summarized as follows:

1. Many claims of special abilities have been found to be fraudulent.

2. Many apparently conclusive experiments supporting ESP have been found to be methodologically flawed.

3. More controlled experimental procedures have failed to demonstrate larger or more reliable ESP effects than did earlier, cruder methods.

4. There is a general lack of consistency in the phenomena, which makes it impossible to move beyond vague theorizing.

Most psychologists remain sceptical about claims in this area, although it is important to keep an open mind. Hansel (1980) published a review of work in this area.

A POSSIBLE PROJECT

You could try investigating the truth of a claim by someone to have telepathic or clairvoyant powers.

There are two basic experimental procedures you could adopt. One involves using the ESP cards described above. The other requires an old shoe box with an end cut out, and a coin.

You need only have one participant to test for clairvoyance, and two (perhaps identical twins, or very close friends) for telepathy.

To demonstrate clairvoyance, the experiment requires the participant to be able to predict what symbol will be on the next ESP card to be turned over. (The experimenter needs to turn their back on the participant, or be in another room to avoid any unintentional cues). In the alternative version of the experiment, the experimenter tosses the coin into the shoebox, without seeing its face, and asks the clairvoyant to predict its face. Matches and mismatches are all recorded for later statistical analysis.

To investigate telepathy a similar procedure is adopted, except that the sender is allowed to see the card, or the face of the coin, and is required to transmit the image to the receiver. Care must be taken here to ensure that no non-verbal communication takes place between the two participants. It may be better to keep them back-to-back, or in adjoining rooms.

If you repeat the procedure many times you may find that a small incidence of 'hits' over the expected average, is actually significant.

What is meant by ESP? Why are most psychologists sceptical about claims of 'special abilities'?

Subliminal Perception

The idea that people can be influenced by messages that are below the usual threshold for perception hit the headlines in 1957 when New Jersey cinema attenders were supposedly influenced by the words 'drink Coca-Cola' and 'eat popcorn'. The furore raised then has not abated with more recent claims that some rock music contains Satanic messages, and erotic images are hidden in advertisements for liquor.

On a more constructive note, perhaps, a whole new industry has developed to help those of us who wish to lose weight, gain confidence, stop smoking, etc., using audiotapes containing subliminal messages. But do these messages work?

Certainly we can perceive stimuli that we are not consciously aware of seeing or hearing or feeling. This has been demonstrated experimentally in as differing areas as guessing weights, preference for photos, and ability to process words. Is this enough to suggest that we can be persuaded subliminally?

It seems likely that because our conscious attention is drawn by the overt stimuli of a visual or auditory presentation (e.g. an advertisement), it will overpower the effect of any subliminal stimuli. More importantly, there has been no reliable evidence to date of the subliminal effect of stimuli to the ear, so the cassette urging you, subliminally, not to eat between meals is unlikely to have any effect on your weight control.

Why do you think people throughout the ages have shown an interest in the paranormal?

ASSIGNMENTS

1. 'Perception is a developmental process'. To what extent does psychological evidence support this statement?

2. 'The context in which a stimulus is perceived is as important as the stimulus itself'. Assess the extent to which psychological evidence supports this view.

FURTHER READING

EYSENCK, M.W. and KEENE, M. (1990) *A Student's Handbook of Cognitive Psychology.* Hove: Erlbaum. [*A readable and comprehensive survey of the current state of cognitive psychology.*]

GREENE, J. and HICKS, C. (1984) *Basic Cognitive Processes.* Milton Keynes: Open University Press. [*In common with most Open University texts this book contains exercises to help you to learn effectively.*]

GREGORY, R.L. (1979) *Eye and Brain.* 3rd ed. New York: McGraw Hill. [*A popular and useful guide to the major areas of visual perception.*]

REDDY, P. (1991) *Attention and Skills Learning.* Leicester: British Psychological Society. [*Another Open Learning Unit which ought to be read in conjunction with this one.*]

REFERENCES

Students studying psychology at pre-degree level, whether in schools, FE colleges or evening institutes, seldom have access to a well-stocked academic library; nor is it expected that they will have consulted all the original references. For most purposes, the books recommended in Further Reading will be adequate. This list is included for the use of those planning a full-scale project on this topic, and also for the sake of completeness.

ALLPORT, G.W. (1955) *Becoming.* New Haven: Yale University Press.

BARBER, P.J. and LEGGE, D. (1976) *Perception and Information.* London: Methuen.

BLAKEMORE, C. and COOPER, G.F. (1970) Development of the brain depends on the visual environment. *Nature,* 228, pp. 477-478.

BOWER, T.R.G. (1966) The visual world of infants. *Scientific American,* 215, pp. 80-92.

BRUCE, V. (1989) The Structure of Faces. In A.W. Young and H.D. Ellis (Eds), *Handbook of Research on Face Processing.* Amsterdam: North Holland.

BRUCE, V. and GREEN, P.R. (1990) *Visual Perception: Physiology, Psychology and Ecology* London: Lawrence Erlbaum Associates, 2nd edition.

BRUNER, J.S. (1957) On perceptual readiness. *Psychological Review,* 64, pp. 123-152.

BRUNER, J.S. and GOODMAN, C.C. (1947) Value and need as organizing factors in perception. *Journal of Abnormal and Social Psychology,* 42, p.33.

CARY, S. and DIAMOND, R. (1977) From piecemeal to configurational representations of faces. *Science,* 195, pp. 312-314.

DEVALOIS, R.L. and DEVALOIS, K.K. (1975) Neural coding of colour. In E.C. Carterette and M.P. Friedman (Eds), *Handbook of perception: Vol. V. Seeing.* New York: Academic Press.

DIAMOND et al. (1983) as cited in ELLIS, H.D. (1990) 'Developmental trends in face recognition'. *The Psychologist,* March 1990.

EYSENCK, M.W., (1984) A *Handbook of Cognitive Psychology.* Hove: Lawrence Erlbaum Associates.

FANTZ, R.L. (1956) A method for studying early visual development. *Perceptual and Motor Skills,* 6, pp. 13-15.

FANTZ, R.L. (1961) The origin of form perception. *Scientific American,* 204, pp. 66-72.

GIBSON, E.J. and WALK, R.D. (1960) The 'visual cliff'. *Scientific American,* 202, pp. 64-71.

GIBSON, E.J. (1969) *Principles of Perceptual Learning and Development.* Englewood Cliffs, N.J: Prentice-Hall.

GIBSON, J.J. (1966) *The Senses Considered as Perceptual Systems.* Boston, Mass: Houghton Mifflin.

GILCHRIST, J.C. and NESBERG, L.S. (1952) Need and perceptual change in need-related objects. *Journal of Experimental Psychology,* 44, p. 369.

GOREN, C.C., SARTY, M. and WU, P.Y.K. (1975). Visual following and pattern discrimination of face-like stimuli by newborn infants. *Pediatrics,* 56, pp. 544-549.

GREGORY, R.L. (1966) *Eye and Brain.* London: Weidenfeld & Nicolson.

GREGORY, R.L. (1972) Seeing as Thinking. *Times Literary Supplement,* June 23.

HAIG, N.D. (1986) Investigating face recognition with an image-processing computer. In H.D. Ellis, M.A. Jeeves, F. Newcombe and A. Young (Eds), *Aspects of Face Processing.* Dordrecht: Martinus Nijhoff.

HAITH, M.M. (1980) *Rules that Babies Look By.* Hillsdale, N.J: Erlbaum.

HANSEL, C.E.M. (1980) *ESP and parapsychology: A critical reevaluation.* Buffalo, NY: Prometheus.

HOCHBERG, J. (1978) *Perception.* Englewood Cliff, N.J: Prentice Hall.

HUBEL, D.H. and WIESEL, T.N. (1979) Brain mechanism of vision. *Scientific American,* (September 1979), pp. 150-162.

JAMES, W. (1890) *The Principles of Psychology.* New York: Holt Rinehart and Winston.

LINDSAY, P.H. and NORMAN, D.A. (1972) *Human Information Processing*. New York: Academic Press.

MARCEL, A. (1983) Conscious and unconscious perception: Experiments in visual masking and word recognition. *Cognitive Psychology*, 15, pp. 197-237.

MARR, D. (1976) Early Processing of Visual Information. *Philosophical Transactions of the Royal Society of London, Series B*, 275, pp. 483-524.

MARR, D. (1982) *Vision: A Computational Investigation into the Human Representation and Processing of Visual Information*. New York: W.H. Freeman.

McGINNIES, E. (1949) Emotionality and perceptual defence. *Psychological Review*, 56, pp. 244-251.

MOSER, P.W. (1987), 'Are cats smart? Yes, at being cats'. *Discover*, May 1987, pp. 77-88.

NAVON, D., (1977) Forest before trees: the precedence of global features in visual perception. *Cognitive Psychology*, 9, pp. 353-383.

NEISSER, U. (1967) *Cognitive Psychology*. New York: Appleton-Century-Crofts.

PALMER, S.E., (1977) Hierarchical Structure in perceptual representation. *Cognitive Psychology*, 9, pp. 441-474.

PERRETT, D.I., HARRIES, M., MISTLIN, A.J. and CHITTY, A.J. (1988) Three stages in the classification of body movements by visual neurons. In H.B. Barlow, C. Blakemore, and M. Weston-Smith (Eds) *Images and Understanding*. Cambridge: Cambridge University Press.

RHINE, J.B. (1942) Evidence of precognition in the covariation of salience. *Journal of Parapsychology*, 6, pp. 111-43.

SALAPATEK, P. (1975) Pattern perception in early infancy. In L.B. Cohen and P. Salapatek (Eds) *Infant Perception: From sensation to cognition* (Vol. 1), New York: Academic Press.

SCHAFER, R. and MURPHY, G. (1974) The role of autism in a visual figure-ground relationship. *Journal of Experimental Psychology*, 32, p. 335.

SENDEN, M.V., (1960) *Space and Sight*. New York: Free Press.

SERGENT, J. (1982) About face: left hemisphere involvement in processing physiognomies. *Journal of Experimental Psychology: Human perception and performance*, 8, pp. 1-4.

STACEY, B., and PIKE, R. (1970) Apparent size, apparent depth and the Müller-Lyer illusion. *Perception and Psychophysics*, 7, pp. 125-128.

WERTHEIMER, M. (1912) Translated in T. Shipley (Ed), *Classics in Psychology*. New York: Philosophical Library, (1961).

WITKIN, H.A., LEWIS, H.B., HERTZMANN, M., MACHORER, K., and WAPNER, S. (1954) *Personality through Perception*. London: Harper & Row.

TURNBULL, C.M. (1961) Some observations regarding the experiences and behaviour of the Bambuti pygmies. *American Journal of Psychology*, 74, pp. 314-318.

WARM, J.S. and DEMBER, W.N. (1986) Awake at the switch. *Psychology Today*, April, pp. 46-53.

GLOSSARY [Terms in bold type also appear as a separate entry]

Absolute threshold: the minimum stimulation which can be detected 50% of the time.

Accommodation: the process by which the lens of the eye varies its focus.

Ambiguous figure: a picture or drawing which is capable of more than one visual interpretation.

Artificial intelligence (AI): an area of research which aims to develop computer systems which will allow the computer to develop novel solutions to problems, or to produce other forms of 'intelligent' behaviour, such as gathering relevant information to aid expert decisions.

Association: learning that one event is associated with another, that relations exist between events.

Binocular cues: depth cues which depend on the use of two eyes.

Bottom-up processing: the picking up of information from the visual stimulus alone.

Colour blindness: detective discrimination of any or all of the colours other than black, white and grey (eg red/green).

Cones: light receptor cells in the retina found largely in the fovea. They are involved in the perception of colour.

Convergence: one of the binocular cues which works as a result of your eyes turning inwards (converging) the closer an object is towards you.

Difference threshold: (*just noticeable difference* or *jnd*): the minimum difference in stimulation that a subject can reliably detect.

Distal stimulus: refers to the object itself which we are looking at. See also *Proximal stimulus*.

Empiricists: the name given to those who believe that perceptions are learned through experience.

Extra-sensory perception: the controversial claim that perception can occur apart from sensory input. It includes clairvoyance, telepathy, precognition and psychokinesis.

Feature detectors: nerve cells in the brain that respond to specific features of a stimulus, such as movement, shape or angle.

Feature theory: one of the pattern recognition theories which assumes that features of a particular stimulus are extracted, combined and compared with a bank of features stored in memory in order to allow pattern recognition.

Field dependent/field independent type: perceptual styles proposed by Witkin. Field independent types are not influenced unduly by the contexts in which objects appear, whereas field dependent types find it difficult to ignore distracting or context cues.

Figure-ground perception: this is the perception of a pattern as the foreground against the background. Even when figure and ground are reversible there is a tendency to perceive one part as figure and the other as ground.

Gestalt principles: these describe how we perceive whole patterns and organize information into meaningful units.

Hering's opponent process theory: see *Opponent process theory (Hering)*.

Illusion: a misrepresentation of the relationships among presented stimuli so that what is perceived does not correspond to physical reality.

jnd (just noticeable difference). See *difference threshold*.

Kinaesthetic sense: the sense of muscles, tendons and joints which provide information about position and movements of parts of the body.

Law of Prägnanz: of several possible organizations one will occur which possesses the best, simplest and most stable shape.

Monocular cues: distance cues such as linear perspective, superimposition etc, which are available to either eye alone.

Motion parallax: a monocular distance cue whereby images of more distant objects move across the retina more slowly than images of nearer objects.

Nativists: those who believe that perception is innately determined.

Nature-nurture debate: one of the major areas of contention in psychology. It considers how much of our behaviour is genetically determined (nature) and how much is due to experience (nurture).

Opponent process theory (Hering): light of a particular wavelength causes a cell to fire more frequently and light of a different wavelength causes it to fire less frequently than its resting rate.

Perceptual constancy: is the process of interpreting an object in an unchanging way despite alterations in light, distance and colour. For example, a Rolls Royce will always be perceived as bigger than a Metro, even if the Rolls Royce is parked further away such that the two retinal images are of identical size.

Perceptual illusion: a misinterpretation of the relationships between parts of a presented stimulus so that what is perceived does not correspond to physical reality.

Perceptual organization: the grouping of low level features of an image into larger structures.

Perceptual set: a mental predisposition to perceive one thing rather than another.

Prototype theory: matching new items to a prototype (best example of a category) to provide the means of classifying items within a perceptual group.

Proximal stimulus: refers to the retinal image of a viewed object. It is from this stimulus rather than the *distal stimulus* that the perceptual system interprets what has been seen.

Psychogalvanic skin response: changes in the electrical conductivity of the skin which may be the result of emotion.

43

Representations: a way of depicting what is taking place in a complex process.

Retinal disparity: a binocular depth cue which depends on the difference between the two retinal images.

Rods: Receptors in the retina which are particularly important in night vision.

Set: see *Perceptual set*.

Signal detection: the ability to respond to the presence of a faint stimulus (the 'signal').

Subliminal perception: occurs when a person is influenced by a stimulus without having been consciously aware of perceiving it.

Template theory: a pattern recognition theory which suggests that we have a number of templates stored in memory against which we compare a new stimulus.

Thalamus: part of the central core of the brain. Directs messages to the sensory receiving areas of the cortex and transmits replies to other areas of the brain.

Top-down processing (conceptually-driven processing): the influence on perception of knowledge and expectation, in addition to stimulus information.

Trichromatic theory (Young-Helmholtz): the theory that there are three types of cone cells which respond to light of a different peak wavelength (corresponding to the red, green and blue regions of the spectrum). Coloured light is made up of a mixture of different wavelengths whose proportions determine the colour of the light.

Visual cliff: an experimental apparatus used to test depth perception in infants and young animals. A sheet of glass covers two patterned surfaces, one immediately below it and the other some distance below it.

Weber's law: states that for a difference between two stimuli to be just noticed, the difference must be some constant proportion of the first stimulus.

Young-Helmholtz trichromatic theory: See *Trichromatic theory (Young-Helmholtz)*.

ANSWERS TO SELF-ASSESSMENT QUESTIONS

SAQ 1 This question checks your understanding of how the visual pathway from eye to brain operates.

Each eye sends information to both hemispheres. The information which is received by the retina closest to the nose channels its information through the optic chiasma to the opposite hemisphere. However, information received on the half of the retina nearest the ears is sent to the hemisphere on the same side as the eye.

It would be useful to refer to Figure 6.

Thus if the right visual cortex were damaged, it would not be able to receive information from that part of the retina closest to the ear of the right eye, but information from the retinal area closest to the nose would still reach the *left* hemisphere. Vision would be restricted, but not lost altogether.

SAQ 2 The Young-Helmholtz Theory suggests that retinal cone cells respond in differing degrees to various colours. This is the first stage of colour processing. What this means is that everything we see is made up of different light wavelengths. There are three types of cone cell, each of which has a peak wavelength, corresponding to red, green and blue regions of the spectrum. Coloured light, which is a combination of these three primary colours, causes the cone cells to respond in proportion to the amount of light reflected from the object. Thus, a Victoria plum which is purple in colour, will cause the red- and blue-sensitive cones to respond most strongly, and the green-sensitive cones to respond very little.

Hering predicted the second stage correctly, where the signals from the retinal cone cells are processed by the nervous system's opponent-process cells on the way to the visual cortex. The opponent process theory involves three different cell types, too, but each cell, according to Hering, will respond in one of two different ways according to the wavelength of the light hitting it.

The three cell types are red/green, blue/yellow and brightness/darkness. This theory explains negative after-effects. If you were to stare at a red light for some time and then look away to a white wall, you would see a green 'light' because green is red's opponent colour.

Hering's theory has been supported by studies on single neurons in the brains of monkeys which show opponent processes taking place (DeValois and DeValois, 1975).

SAQ 3 A cat with only one eye would be quite capable of catching its prey because there are 8 different distance cues available to monocular vision. These are:

   (i) Relative size — the further an object is away from the eye, the smaller will be the image on the retina.

   (ii) Relative brightness — the brighter objects are perceived as closer to us; hazier objects are perceived as more distant.

   (iii) Superimposition — objects which block out part or all of another image are seen as closer.

   (iv) Height in the visual field — if one object is higher in the visual field it is perceived as more distant.

   (v) Texture gradient — elements of an image, such as pebbles on a beach or blades of grass, show an apparent gradient in the size of image of each element as the surface recedes.

   (vi) Linear and aerial perspective — parallel lines appear to converge as they recede into the distance.

   (vii) Motion parallax — as you move, images of more distant objects travel across the retina more slowly.

   (viii) Accommodation — this physiological cue works for distances up to about 4 feet. The lens changes shape to keep the image of an object on the retina in the sharpest focus.

All this means that the cat can cope. However, there are two very important cues which are not available to animals (or humans) who only have one eye, since these depend on some interaction between the two eyes.

   (ix) Retinal disparity — refers to the fact that the two retinal images are slightly different. These two images are superimposed to give further depth cues.

   (x) Convergence — if an object is more than about 25 feet away your two eyes will have an almost parallel line of vision. Anything less than this and the eyes will turn inwards, towards the object.

We can see then, that the cat will be capable of catching prey, though not as effectively as another cat with two eyes.

SAQ 4 This question covers much the same ground as SAQ 3 although the emphasis is slightly different. It is expecting evidence concerning the interactive effects of the two eyes in retinal disparity and convergence, which provide the 'fine tuning' of distance perception.

If you have undertaken the project comparing monocular and binocular viewing conditions you will have a graphic illustration of just how important two eyes are to the accuracy perception of distance. This practical exercise demonstrates the usefulness of two eyes more than any number of theoretical explanations.

SAQ 5 There is ample scope here for a range of responses. Any 5 of the following would be acceptable. You should be able to explain how each example contributes to making sense of the world.

   — law of proximity
   — law of closure
   — law of good continuation
   — law of similarity
   — figure and ground
   — shape constancy
   — size constancy
   — lightness constancy
   — colour constancy
   — location constancy.

SAQ 6 Gregory's explanation of the Müller-Lyer illusion involved the use of depth and distance cues. If we apply these to the Ponzo illusion, we have to think of something like a railway track. The two incoming vertical lines resemble the track itself and the lines in the middle remind us of wooden or concrete sleepers. Size constancy tells us that things which are the same size will appear smaller as they recede from view, and so the top line must be smaller.

In addition, we know that height in the visual field is also a cue to distance. Items which are higher in the visual field are further away, and again we are led into thinking that the top line must be shorter.

SAQ 7 You were asked to consider only 3 theories, but the extra notes are given here as this SAQ could provide the basis for an essay.

Gestalt theories — the Law of Prägnanz, including:
   — law of proximity
   — law of closure
   — law of good continuation
   — law of similarity
   — figure and ground

Evaluation of Gestalt theories:
   — give an insight into the assumptions about the world upon which our visual system is based.

45

— no information provided about how the brain processes the information on the retina into separate objects.
— Navon (1977) — overall forms of patterns are analyzed before individual components.
— Palmer (1977) — analysis of forms is hierarchical, moving from the overall configuration down to basic elements.

Perceptual constancies:
— shape
— size
— lightness
— colour
— location

Perceptual illusions:
— use these only to show how they have helped to explain the processes involved in perceptual organization — Gregory's explanations and Stacey and Pike's challenge should be considered here.

Pattern recognition theories — brief explanation (including the limitations) of:
— template theory
— prototype theory
— feature theory.

Marr's computational theory:
— a consideration of the what, why and how of the functions of visual perception.

Evaluation of Marr:
— involves a blending of physiology, psychology and artificial intelligence.

WARNING!!
You need to be careful not to write a descriptive essay along the lines of 'All I know about Gestalt principles, visual illusions, etc'. Such an essay will not fulfil the criteria for this question as there will be no *evaluation*. The likelihood is that such an essay will gain something like 10 out of 25, no matter how well it is presented.

SAQ 8 This question would permit any 5 of the following:

— motivation
— instructions
— context
— expectations
— cultural factors
— reward and punishment
— emotion
— (past) experience
— (individual) differences.

For each chosen bias you need to point out how it results in only some features of the stimulus being noticed.

EG: *Context is influential because it works in tandem with expectations to determine what you anticipate seeing next. When you are attending a psychology lecture, you would not be surprised to be addressed by the Professor of Psychology of your local University. You would not expect a pop star to be speaking to you. The pop star would be out of context, and so might take longer to be recognized.*

SAQ 9 This is one of the major areas of debate in psychology: whether our behaviour is genetically endowed or the result of environmental factors such as learning.

The nativists take the position that we are born with our perceptual abilities, whereas the empiricists argue that our perceptual abilities are the result of experience.

SAQ 10 The Gibson and Walk 'visual cliff' experiments were criticized as failing to prove that depth perception was innate because the youngest babies they used were 6 months. (Any younger than this and the babies would have been unable to crawl.) Even though this is very young some experience and learning about the world has taken place, and therefore it could not be conclusively stated that the perception of depth was an innate response.

SAQ 11 Evidence for the nativists' position:
— Fantz (1956) visual preferences.
— Salapatek (1975) — systematic scanning of the visual world by babies as young as 6 weeks.
— Gibson (1969) — 4 basic perceptual strategies which children tend to move through from infancy to adolescence.
— Bower (1966) — shape perception in 2-month-old babies.
— Gibson and Walk (1960) — visual cliff experiments with infants 6-14 months old.
— Goren, Sarty and Wu (1975) — babies with mean age of 9 minutes preferred to follow a schematic face rather than a blank head shape.

Criticisms:
— most of the research involves babies who, although young, have had some experience of the world, and therefore it is hard to separate the learned and innate responses.

Evidence for the empiricists' position:
— animal deprivation studies such as Blakemore and Cooper (1970) show that the deprivation of some visual experiences leads to a permanent loss of abilities. This suggests experience is necessary for normal development.
— Senden (1960) — human adult cataract patients who have had their sight surgically restored did not recover all their visual functions.

Criticisms:
— it is hard to generalize from animal studies to humans.
— adult-restored vision is problematic since we never know whether or not parts of the visual system have deteriorated after years of disuse.
— despite years of blindness, cataract patients have been accumulating years of experience about the visual world to maximize any residual vision they have, and they have been learning about the world through their other senses.
— we should be careful in generalizing from adult-restored vision to the newborn's visual system.

Conclusion:
— seems most reasonable to accept that children are born into the world with the capacity for visual perception but specific discriminations require specific experiences.

SAQ 12 ESP stands for extra-sensory perception or the ability to perceive things without using our 5 senses. The four areas associated with ESP are:

— telepathy
— clairvoyance
— precognition
— psychokinesis.

The reasons for scepticism about claims for ESP are:

(i) Many claims have been found to be fraudulent.

(ii) So-called decisive experiments have been methodologically flawed.

(iii) Tighter experimental procedures have failed to demonstrate more reliable ESP effects.

(iv) There is a lack of consistency about the phenomena.